MORE DRAWINGS

DOVER PUBLICATIONS, INC.

NEW YORK

BY HEINRICH KLEY

Published in Canada by General Publishing Company, Ltd., 30 Lesmill Road, Don Mills, Toronto,
Ontario.
Published in the United Kingdom by Constable
and Company, Ltd., 10 Orange Street, London WC 2.

This Dover edition, first published in 1962, is a
selection of drawings from the following two books:
Leut' und Viecher, published by Albert Langen
in 1912.
Sammel-Album, published by Albert Langen in
1923.
More Drawings by Heinrich Kley comprises all
the illustrations in the above-mentioned books ex-
cept those which duplicate illustrations in *Skizzenbuch* (1909) and *Skizzenbuch II* (1910), which
are published by Dover Publications under the
title *The Drawings of Heinrich Kley*.

Library of Congress Catalog Card Number: 62-5906

Manufactured in the United States of America
Dover Publications, Inc.
180 Varick Street
New York, N.Y. 10014

A Pair of Butterflies
Das Schmetterlingspärchen

1

The Family at the Seashore
Familienbad

Silver Wedding
Silberhochzeit

Here Lies Anonymous
Hier ruht in Gott N.N.

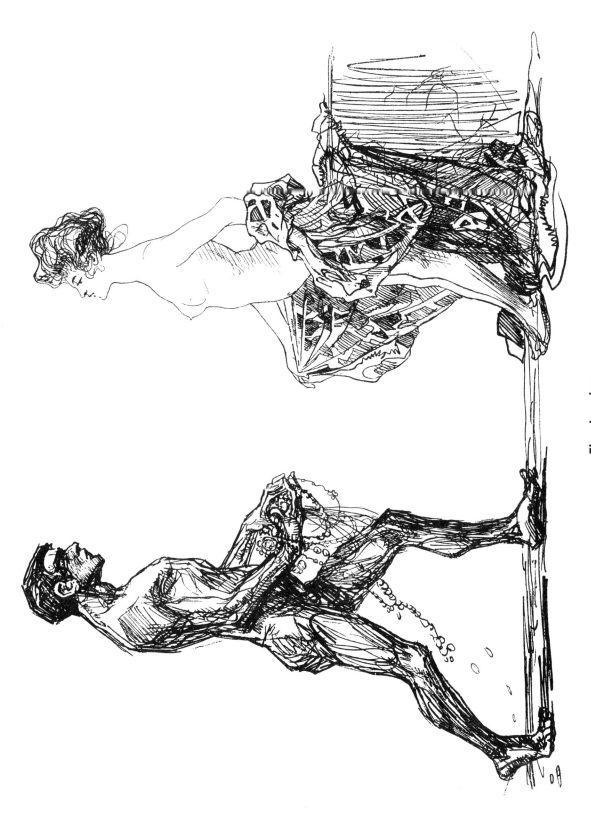

The Jeweler
Der Juwelier

School Bench
Schulbank

Strong Tobacco
Starker Tobak

Caterpillars and Butterflies
Raupen und Schmetterlinge

Interior View
Interieur

Clearing the Field
Feldbereinigung

14

Lent
Fastenzeit

The Pickpocket
Der Taschendieb

The Caterpillar's Meal
Raupenfrass

18

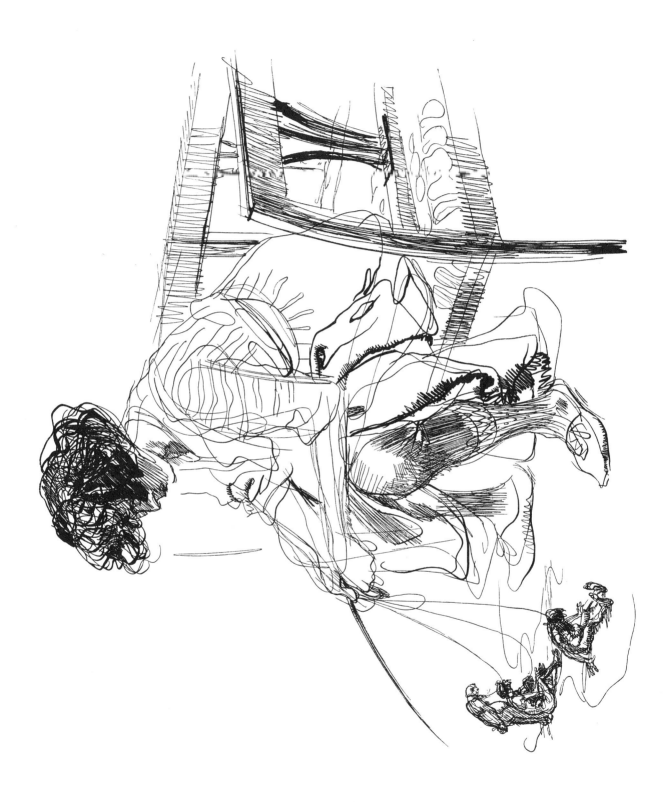

20

*Odol is the trade name of a German mouthwash.

Fiddle Bow and Sounding Box
Fiedelbogen und Resonanzkasten

Get out!
Nu aber raus!

*The sign reads: "Paradise—picture-taking forbidden" (Paradies—Photographiren verboten).

24

25

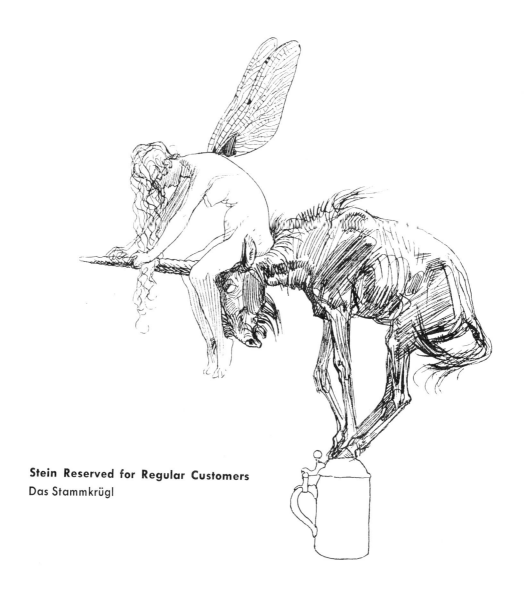

Stein Reserved for Regular Customers
Das Stammkrügl

The Apostles
Die Jünger

The Ridge
Der Grat

All Souls' Day
Allerseelen

The Raisins in the Cake
Die Rosinen im Kuchen

Testing for Stress and Strain
Die Belastungsprobe

The Schnaps Bottle
Die Schnapsbuddel

32

To be or not to be . . .
Sein oder nicht sein . . .

Waltz on the Ice
Eiswalzer

Blessed with Children
Der Kindersegen

In the Churchyard
Auf dem Kirchhof

**She sang to him, she spoke to him:
His end was certain then**

Sie sang zu ihm, sie sprach zu ihm:
Da war's um ihn geschehn

**She drew him in, he sank within—
Was never seen again!**

Halb zog sie ihn, halb sank er hin—
Und ward nicht mehr gesehn!

*The quotation is from Goethe's poem "Der Fischer" ("The Fisherman").

Cherry Blossom Time
Blütenschnee

38

The Fire Brigade
Die Feuerwehr

Minimax
Minimax

*Minimax is the trade name of a popular German fire extinguisher.

Anatomy and Palace Chapel
Anatomie und Schlosskapelle

43

*The left-hand sign reads: "Close-out sale at any price—religious articles" (Ausverkauf zu jedem Preis— Devotionaler Handlung). The right-hand sign reads: "Paris novelties, genuine English originals" (Pariser Nuwote, ächt englisch Original).

One-horse Coach
Einspänner

He Loves Me, He Loves Me Not
Blumenorakel

Strike of the Milk Cows

Streik der Milchkühe

46

At Nature's Breast
An der Brust der Natur

47

Picnic
Picknick

The Snaps
Die Druckknöpfe

The Patient German

Der gute Michel

Honorable Approaches
Ehrbare Annäherung

53

54

Punch on New Year's Eve
Sylvesterpunsch

The Demon Alcohol
Der Alkoholteufel

The Course
Die Strecke

*The German caption contains a pun on two meanings of *Strecke*, "course" and "bag" (in hunting).

Highway Toll
Pflasterzoll

*The letter reads: "Dear Fanny, Yesterday I got done with my ship screw wings . . ." (Liebe Fanny, Gestern bin ich mit meinen Schiffsschraubenflügeln fertig geworden . . .).

Adagio
Adagio

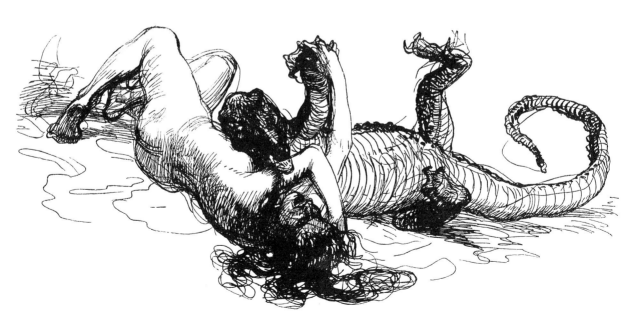

Ground-floor Acrobatics
Parterre-Akrobatik

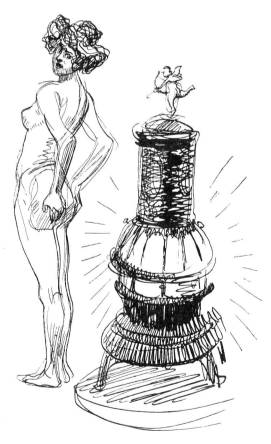

Slow-combustion Burner
Permanentbrenner

Springtime
Im Maien

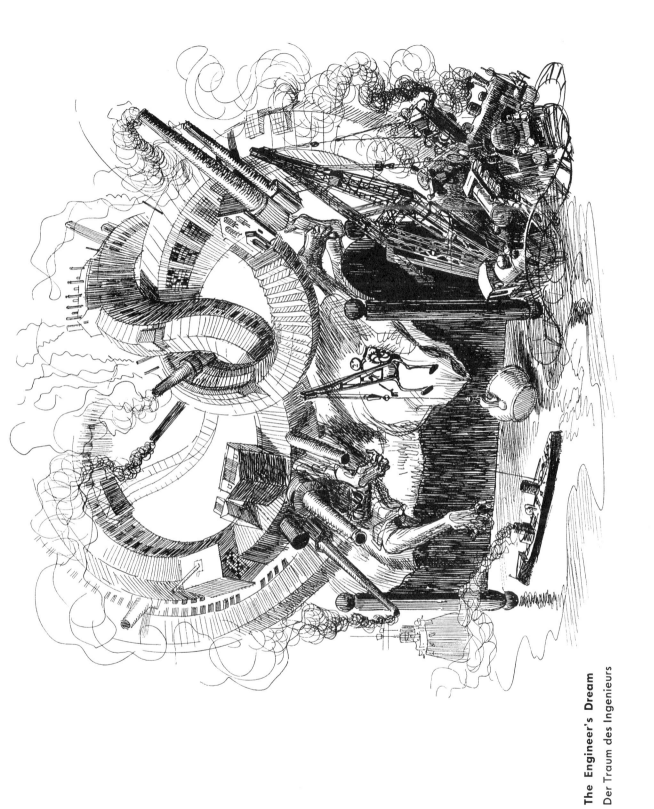

The Engineer's Dream
Der Traum des Ingenieurs

67

Revelation
Enthüllung

The Summer Hiker
Der Sommerfrischler

*The sign on the bench reads: "Society for Beautification (Verschönerungs-Verein), Neuhaus-Schliersee."

The Dangerous Age
Das gefährliche Alter

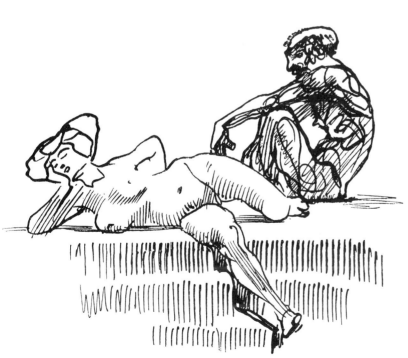

The Joys of Skiing

Skikjöring

Art Criticism

Kunstkritik

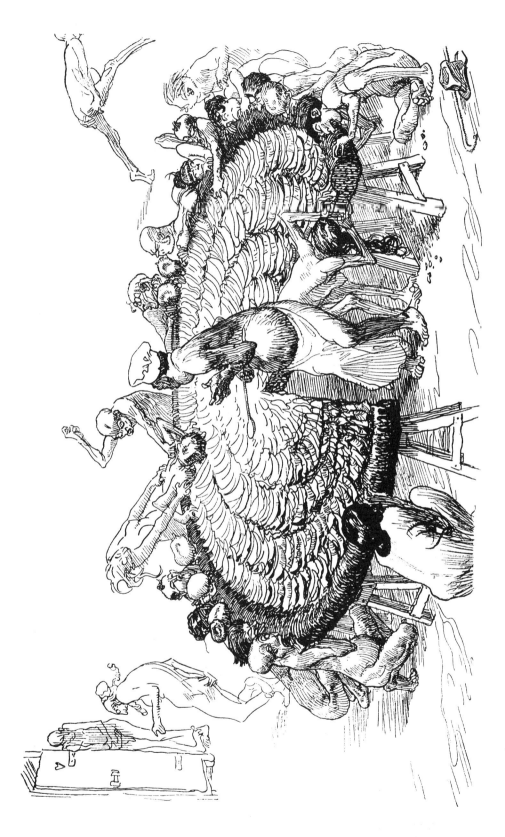

The Prune Tart
Der Zwetschgen-Kuchen

"I want to carve it in every bark"

"Ich schnitt es gern in alle Rinden ein"

*The quotation is from Schubert's "Ungeduld" (part of *Die Schöne Müllerin* song cycle), words by Wilhelm Müller.

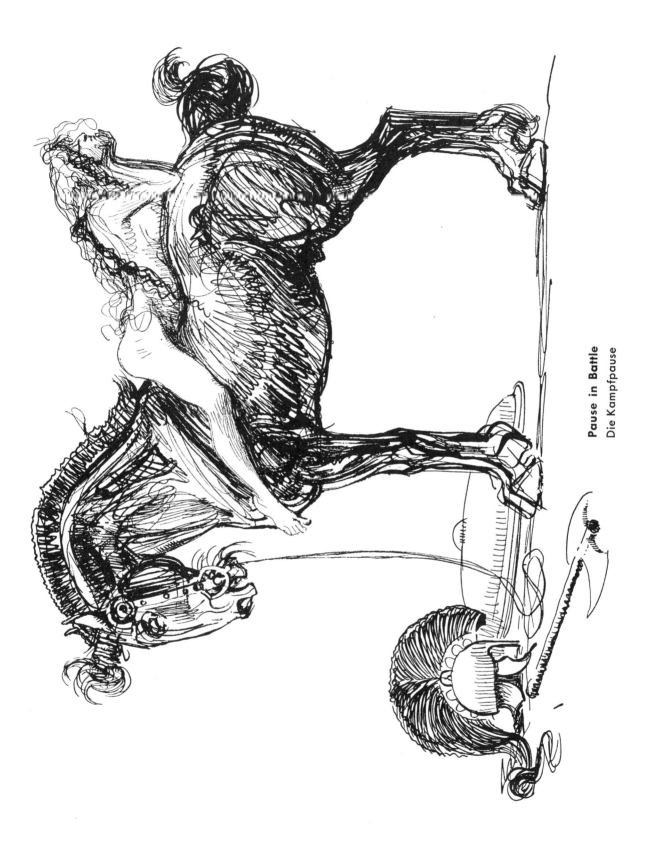

Pause in Battle
Die Kampfpause

78

Woodruff
Waldmeister

*Woodruff is an herb used for flavoring May wine.

79

The Spill
Der Fidibus

Gout
Das Zipperlein

White Slave Trader
Der Mädchenhändler

Ladies' Choice (at a dance)
Damenwahl

Education for Marriage
Die Erziehung zur Ehe

Easter Eggs
Ostereier

Guided Tour
Fremdenrundfahrt

May Wine

Maibowle

The Easter Bunny

Der Osterhase

Gathering Grapes
Die Weinlese

The Wine-Press
Die Weinkelter

Starched Linen
Stärkwäsche

Rococo
Rokoko

At the Hofbräu
Im Hofbräu

92

The Checkroom
In der Garderobe

93

The Ski-jump
Der Sprunghügel

The Iconoclasts
Die Bilderstürmer

Pinching Cure

Kneippkur

*The German caption contains a pun on *kneipen* (to pinch) and Dr. Kneipp, who developed a severe cold-water cure which is even now widely popular.

Dream Dancers
Traumtänzerinnen

Celery Roots
Sellerieknollen

Snow Clearing
Die Schneeräumer

Poppy Day
Heckenröschentag

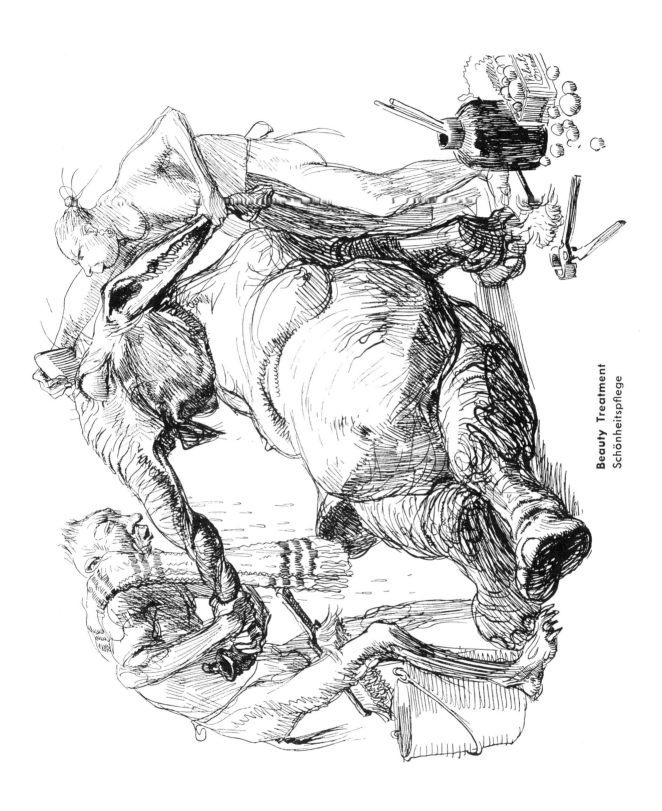

Beauty Treatment
Schönheitspflege

"Smile, please!"
"Bitte recht freundlich!"

Dover Books on Art

THE DRAWINGS OF HEINRICH KLEY. Uncut publication of long-sought-after sketchbooks of satiric, ironic iconoclast. Remarkable fantasy, weird symbolism, brilliant technique make Kley a shocking experience to layman, endless source of ideas, techniques for artist. 200 drawings, captions translated. Introduction. 136pp. 6 x 9.　　　　　T24 Paperbound $1.85

FOOT-HIGH LETTERS: A GUIDE TO LETTERING, M. Price. 28 15½ x 22½" plates, give classic Roman alphabet, one foot high per letter, plus 9 other 2" high letter forms for each letter. 16 page syllabus. Ideal for lettering classes, home study. 28 plates in box.　　　　　T239 $6.00

A HANDBOOK OF WEAVES, G. H. Oelsner. Most complete book of weaves, fully explained, differentiated, illustrated. Plain weaves, irregular, double-stitched, filling satins; derivative, basket, rib weaves; steep, broken, herringbone, twills, lace, tricot, many others. Translated, revised by S. S. Dale; supplement on analysis of weaves. Bible for all handweavers. 1875 illustrations. 410pp. 6⅛ x 9¼.　　　　　T209 Clothbound $5.00

JAPANESE HOMES AND THEIR SURROUNDINGS, E. S. Morse. Classic describes, analyses, illustrates all aspects of traditional Japanese home, from plan and structure to appointments, furniture, etc. Published in 1886, before Japanese architecture was contaminated by Western, this is strikingly modern in beautiful, functional approach to living. Indispensable to every architect, interior decorator, designer. 307 illustrations. Glossary. 410pp. 5⅝ x 8⅜.　　　　　T746 Paperbound $2.00

DESIGN FOR ARTISTS AND CRAFTSMEN, L. Wolchonok. The most thorough course on the creation of art motifs and designs. Shows you step-by-step, with hundreds of examples and 113 detailed exercises, how to create original designs from geometric patterns, plants, birds, animals, humans, and man-made objects. "A great contribution to the field of design and crafts," N. Y. SOCIETY OF CRAFTSMEN. More than 1300 entirely new illustrations. xv + 207pp. 7⅞ x 10¾.
　　　　　T274 Clothbound $4.95

HANDBOOK OF DESIGNS AND DEVICES, C. P. Hornung. A remarkable working collection of 1836 basic designs and variations, all copyright-free. Variations of circle, line, cross, diamond, swastika, star, scroll, shield, many more. Notes on symbolism. "A necessity to every designer who would be original without having to labor heavily," ARTIST AND ADVERTISER. 204 plates. 240pp. 5⅜ x 8.　　　　　T125 Paperbound $1.90

THE UNIVERSAL PENMAN, George Bickham. Exact reproduction of beautiful 18th century book of handwriting. 22 complete alphabets in finest English roundhand, other scripts, over 2000 elaborate flourishes, 122 calligraphic illustrations, etc. Material is copyright-free. "An essential part of any art library, and a book of permanent value," AMERICAN ARTIST. 212 plates. 224pp. 9 x 13¾.　　　　　T20 Clothbound $10.00

THE HANDBOOK OF PLANT AND FLORAL ORNAMENT,
R. G. Hatton. 1200 line illustrations, from medieval, Renaissance herbals, of flowering or fruiting plants: garden flowers, wild flowers, medicinal plants, poisons, industrial plants, etc. A unique compilation that probably could not be matched in any library in the world. Formerly "The Craftman's Plant-Book." Also full text on uses, history as ornament, etc. 548pp. 6⅛ x 9¼.

T649 Paperbound $2.98

METHODS AND MATERIALS OF THE GREAT SCHOOLS AND MASTERS, Sir Charles Eastlake. (Formerly titled "Materials for a History of Oil Painting".) Vast, authentic reconstruction of secret techniques of the masters, recreated from ancient manuscripts, contemporary accounts, analysis of paintings, etc. Oils, fresco, tempera, varnishes, encaustics. Both Flemish and Italian schools, also British and French. One of great works for art historians, critics; inexhaustible mine of suggestions, information for practicing artists. Total of 1025pp. 5⅜ x 8.

Two volume set, T718-9 Paperbound $4.00

VASARI ON TECHNIQUE, G. Vasari. Pupil of Michelangelo, outstanding biographer of Renaissance artists reveals technical methods of his day. Marble, bronze, fresco painting, mosaics, engraving, stained glass, rustic ware, etc. Only English translation, extensively annotated by G. Baldwin Brown. 18 plates. 342pp. 5⅜ x 8.

T717 Paperbound $2.00

COSTUMES OF THE ANCIENTS, Thomas Hope. Beautiful, clear, sharp line drawings of Greek and Roman figures in full costume, by noted artist and antiquary of early 19th century. Dress, armor, divinities, masks, etc. Invaluable sourcebook for costumers, designers, first-rate picture file for illustrators, commercial artists. Introductory text by Hope. 300 plates. 6 x 9.

T21 Paperbound $2.00

VITRUVIUS: TEN BOOKS ON ARCHITECTURE. The most influential book in the history of architecture. 1st century A.D. Roman classic has influenced such men as Bramante, Palladio, Michelangelo, up to present. Classic principles of design, harmony, etc. Fascinating reading. Definite English translation by Professor H. Morgan, Harvard. 334pp. 5⅜ x 8.

T645 Paperbound $2.00

Dover publishes books on commercial art, art history, crafts, design, art classics; also books on music, literature, science, mathematics, puzzles and entertainments, chess, engineering, biology, philosophy, psychology, languages, history, and other fields. For free circulars write to Dept. DA, Dover Publications, Inc., 180 Varick St., New York 14, N.Y.